David Roberts

David Roberts was born in Stockbridge, Edinburgh in 1796. He was apprenticed for seven years to a painter and decorator, during which time he studied art in the evenings. Roberts started work as a professional scene painter at the Theatre Royal, Edinburgh in 1822. In the same year, he showed three of his architectural pictures in the Exhibition of Living Artists. Soon he moved to London to the sceneroom of Covent Garden.

After his first trip to the Continent, his reputation was made when he exhibited his collection of drawings. By 1826 he was able to leave the theatrical world, and concentrate on art, selling and exhibiting his works, until in 1831 he was elected President of the Society of British Artists.

Several years later he made an extended journey to the Middle East — sketching and painting. He became sick with "intermittent fever", thought to have been brought on by the severe privations that he endured during his journeys. On his return to England, his drawings created a sensation. The originality of the places he had discovered caused great excitement and widespread interest in the world of art of his day. He became an R.A. in 1841 and was honoured with the Freedom of the City of Edinburgh in 1858.

During his lifetime he painted some 260 oil paintings — many of which can be seen today in the London Museums. He died in 1864 and is buried in Norwood cemetery.

Cleopatra's Needle

The most striking monuments of ancient Alexandria are the well known Obelisks and Pompey's Pillar. ....These Obelisks stood originally at Heliopolis, and were brought to Alexandria by one of the Caesars, perhaps Julius, since tradition has attached to them the title of Cleopatra's Needles. They are of red granite of Syene.... the standing Obelisk is about seventy-five feet high, and seven feet seven inches square at its base.

Pompey's Pillar — Alexandria

This relic of antiquity is the first object seen in approaching Alexandria, from the sea, on the coast of Egypt. "It stands on an eminence about 1800 feet to the south of the present walls." .....The proper name of this column has been much questioned. The murder of Pompey on the coast of Egypt probably led to the original error that it was his cenotaph : but the successful deciphering of an almost obliterated inscription on the pedestal shows that it was erected by Publius, a Prefect of Egypt, in honour of Diocletian.

Side view of the Great Sphinx

The mutilated state of this enormous figure is, perhaps more strikingly observed in profile than in front.......undisturbed possession of its solitude is left to the Great Sphinx, the most extraordinary of the productions of man in this land of his wonders. After drawing and studying it, Mr. Roberts said that he had had more powerful emotions excited by it than by the Pyramids.......That the Sphinx was worshipped, there is no doubt; an altar was found before the Temple, erected between its paws.

Pyramids of Geezeh (Gizah) from the Nile

When the river is low and the intersecting canals dry and practicable, the journey from Grand Cairo to the Pyramids of Geezeh is a ride of little more than an hour. The traveller mounts in the streets of New Cairo, and rides to Old Cairo, where he crosses the Nile at the Madiah, or ferry, to a village the nearest to the Pyramids, though five miles distant from them, called Geezeh, whence the association of its name with these wonders of Egypt and the world. From across the Nile the appearance of these stupendous constructions is that which is here represented.

General View of Cairo from the West

....The walls of Cairo were originally built of brick, and continued in the same state till the reign of the celebrated Saladin; but there are in the circuit some towers that appear to be of Roman origin....... The citadel ...... appears on the left of our drawing; its commanding and impregnable situation fits it for the arsenal, the Pasha's palace, and other buildings which require security. ....Between the extreme left of this view.... and the vast Mosque of the Sultan Hassan, lies the large square or place called the Roumelia. The Pyramids of Geezeh, the most striking objects in Egypt, are seen, beyond the Nile...... All and everything is Oriental in the scene − the flat roofs of the dwellings, the handsome domes, and the numerous and elegant minarets of the mosques.......

Citadel of Cairo, the Residence of the Pasha

This striking view is taken from a ruined mosque near the city walls, and looking towards the rock of the Citadel, which stretches along the horizon.......Between the observer and the hill of the Citadel lies the great nercopolis of Cairo..... in which the dead of ages are laid, and where those splendid religious edifices are found which are commonly called the Tombs of the Sultans. The ruined mosque in the foreground is built in an angle of the city wall. From one of the gates below a caravan is seen issuing......It may be easily imagined how very fine the view of Cairo and the surrounding country must be from those accessible points of the Citadel which complete a panoramic survey..:.....where the city is seen below the observer, with its thousand minarets and domes; and the valley of the Nile is commanded from the Great Pyramids and those of Saccara on the South, and towards the north, to its subsidence into the Delta.

The Ghawázees, or dancing girls of Cairo

The Ghawázees are dancing girls who perform unveiled in the public streets......their dances have little elegance and less decorum. Their dress is similar to that worn by the middle classes in Egypt. They often perform in the court of a house, or in the street before the door, on occasions of festivity, such as a marriage or the birth of a child; ....They are often extremely handsome, and among them are certainly to be found the finest women in Egypt. Their origin is certainly involved in great obscurity, resembling in some points another mysterious people, the gipsies........They still keep themselves distinct from other classes and abstain from marriages except with persons of their own tribe: they have a peculiar language, too, which they use to conceal their communications from strangers.

Entrance to the Caves of Beni Hassan

This portico to the catacombs is remarkable, as it probably illustrated the origin of the Doric order of the Greeks.....at a very remote period, at least 1500 B.C., and, therefore, earlier than any known Greek temple.....

The great interest, however....lies in the pictorial representations left by the ancient Egyptians on the walls of these catacombs....the arts, habits, and pursuits of the Egyptians, in their social state, are painted. Here they are represented occupied in their various trades, as potters, weavers, glass-blowers......their sports are shown in dancing, music,......playing with balls and at chess......The chase of wild animals, fowling and fishing agricultural pursuits, planting, sowing, reaping......the management of herds and flocks...... The caves of Beni Hassan have, in short, preserved the best, and in many cases the only information we possess, of the manners, pursuits, and customs of this extraordinary people.

Portico of the Temple of Dendera

These magnificent ruins are situated on the western plain of the valley of the Nile, ...The Portico of the Temple is lofty enough to be seen from the river. The state of its preservation is remarkable, for the parts uninjured by violence are as sharp in the sculpture and as vivid in the painting as if they were recently executed; but force has been used to obliterate the features of the goddess, to whose worship the Temple was dedicated......these injuries were done, most probably, by the Iconoclasts upon the introduction of Christianity into the valley of the Nile;......Though it is the most recent of the Egyptian temples, for it was begun at the commencement of the Christian era, still, from its magnitude and beauty, it is scarcely less imposing, and not less beautiful, than other celebrated remains of an earlier and more glorious period of Egyptian history.

Hadjar Silsilis, or the Rock of the Chain (Feluccas on the Nile)

The view is taken looking down the river; and it will be seen that the rocks are much higher on the right, or eastern, than on the western bank. .....The lofty cliffs are composed of a rock of fine and continuous texture, admirably fitted for the purpose to which it has been so largely applied. The quarries extend two or three miles along the river..... Some of the excavations are six hundred feet long, three hundred feet wide, and from seventy to eighty feet high; but they nowhere appear to have been worked below the level of the Nile. ....The durability of the sandstone of these quarries is shown not only in the fine and sharp work executed on the columns, walls and entablatures of the temples, and where, ...the forms left by the sculptor are still preserved, but in the quarries where the stones were hewn, the splinters lie about as fresh in appearance, ..."as if the labourer had left his work only the evening before and might be expected to return and resume it, but that evening was two thousand years ago."

A Colossal Statue at the Entrance to the Temple of Luxor

This mutilated figure is one of the two sitting statues which were placed before the grand propylon of the Temple of Luxor, one on either side of the entrance; they are of granite, and, though seated, they must have been nearly fifty feet in height.....These figures represent Remeses II......The faces have been entirely disfigured by violence, or we should probably have found.....some of the finest examples of Egyptian sculpture, for they were of that period which was the most distinguished for art in Egypt. They bear on their heads the double caps, the mitre surmounting the corn-measure, as evidence of his sovereignty in Upper and Lower Egypt.

Grand Entrance to the Temple of Luxor

"How beautiful, how grand the approach to Luxor must have been......" This sketch is made from the summit of a mound that overlooks the huts of the village of Luxor; ....it is here that the vast propylon and the remaining Obelisk, ...are best seen. ....The propyla are enriched with elaborate sculpture, recording the military deeds and conquests of Remeses II. ......The perforations or openings seen in these propyla, and the grooves or steps immediately below, were for affixing the flag-staffs, on which floated the banners on the days of ceremony.

One only of the colossal statues of Remeses is seen between the Obelisk and the propylon; the other is concealed in this view: .....Over the left propylon appears the top of the minaret of the Mosque of Abd Alhajaj. Whilst our Artist was sketching, a hawk — a descendant of those from whom Osiris was symbolised — perched sometimes on the Obelisk, and occasionally swept down upon the pigeons, collected in such infinite numbers around him.

At Luxor: Thebes

The beautiful subject of this vignette, taken from that extremity of the Temple which is the nearest to the Nile, is almost the only part of it which is free from the.......mud habitations "in the midst of the lordly halls of the Pharaohs, ..."

"The capitals are supposed to have had their forms suggested by the budding lotus; ... the whole is crowned with a square block or abacus."

General View of Karnak, looking towards Bab'an-El-Molook

In this view, looking towards the north, the eye commands the whole of the ruins of the Great Temple of Karnak, and ranges from the farthest extremity, beyond the wall of circumvallation, over its most sacred precincts, to the entrance facing the Nile; passing by its obelisks, through its stupendous Hall of Columns, and across its vast courts, to the enormous masses of masonry which compose its great propylon: ....Where busy millions have trod, all is now decayed and desolate; leaving only as a record of the greatness of its Pharaohs, structures so vast, even in their ruins, that nothing exists in any other country, within thousands of years of the age of their erection, to mark such power and greatness in any other former age and people........"From the desert to the river, from within or without, by sunshine or by moonlight — however you contemplate Karnak — appears the very aspect in which it shows to most advantage.......And when all this was perfect...... when its courts were paced by gorgeous priestly pageants, and busy life swarmed on a river flowing between banks of palaces......when all this was in its prime, no wonder that its fame spread even over the barbarian world, and found immortality in Homer's song."

General View of the Ruins of Karnak, from the West

This view, which embraces the whole range and extent of these stupendous ruins, is taken, looking towards the east at sunrise, from the summit of a small temple that is situated near it. On the extreme left.....rises the great propylon to which an approach from the Nile was made.....At nearly right angles, lay another approach, through an avenue of sphinxes, supposed to have extended from Luxor; of this avenue traces are here seen.....through a second propylon and a magnificent though ruined gateway, lies the entrance to the grand Hall of Columns — a structure which in extent and vastness, has no parallel in the world...

Thebes — The Colossal Statues of Amunoph III

The view of these wonders of the plains of Thebes is taken from the upper or southern side of the group. These enormous figures rest where they did at the period of their erection, when they formed the entrance of a grand dromos to the Temple, 1100 feet in length. A line of hieroglyphics extends from the shoulder down the back to the pedestal, and here is found the name of the Pharaoh whom the statue represented, Amunoph III. The figures seen climbing up the throne of the vocal Memnon are Messrs. Hurnard and Corry, who were at that time Mr. Robert's travelling companions.

Entrance to the Tombs of the Kings — Bab'an-El-Molook

Here the Pharaohs of Thebes were entombed, in a narrow valley......These tombs were most costly in their construction, penetrating into the rocks to great depths, and enriched with the most elaborate appliances of art. It is difficult to conceive why such lavish expenditure was incurred in places ingeniously contrived for concealment.........The plains below once teemed with life, and, perhaps swarmed with palaces: but the gloomy defiles.......must have been, as they now are, lonely, lifeless, desolate, − a fit avenue to the tombs.......

Fragment of the Great Colossus at the Memnonium, Thebes

This fragment of the Temple, ...of circular columns, with capitals of the budding lotus, is a beautiful and picturesque object. The fragment of a statue of Remeses II is, however, the great wonder of the memnonium. ....It was formed of one stupendous mass of syenite, or granite.......and represented the king seated on a throne, with his hands resting on his knees. ....It has now been overthrown, and the colossal fragments lie scattered round the pedestal. If it be a matter of surprise how the Egyptians could transport and erect a mass of such dimensions, the means employed to destroy it are scarcely less extraordinary.....No idea can be conveyed of its gigantic size, it probably exceeded, when entire, nearly three times the solid contents of the great obelisk at Karnak, and weighed nearly nine hundred tons.

Medinet Abou, Thebes

These ruins are situated on the western bank of the Nile, in the plain which everywhere within the precincts of ancient Thebes exhibits indications of that vast city. .... The portico seen in front is of a comparitively late date, and built out of the ruins of ancient structures: .... The taller tower-like building......... is part of the palace of Remeses IV, of which the square openings are the windows of small chambers, decorated with elegant sculptures of domestic subjects, that illustrate the habits and manners of the ancient Egyptians. .... The brick walls and mounds seen to surround the Temple are the ruins of the houses of the Christian population, which once enlivened this spot: now all is desolate.

Interior of the Temple of Esne, (Esna) in Upper Egypt

There is scarcely a more beautiful example than this Temple of the Ptolemaic period of Egyptian architecture......The walls in front of the portico are seen on the left, ...the door in the centre, by which it is entered, is level with the external ground, and from it a flight of steps descends to the floor of the portico.......In this transverse view one half of the portico only is seen: the whole has six columns in width, and four in depth. Whilst Mr. Roberts was in the portico some Copts....observed his sketching....and recognised in him a Christian brother by crossing themselves whenever they addressed him.

Temple of Edfou (Edfu), Ancient Apollinopolis, Upper Egypt

....Even in its state of ruin, the great Temple is one of the most entire in Egypt.....The period of its erection is comparatively modern: it was begun by Ptolemy Philometer about 160 years B.C., and carried on to completion through the next two reigns......The situation is in the midst of a plain naturally fertile, ...the Temple lies about five miles from the Nile, which is seen in the distance, and beyond it appears the ridge of mountains where the ancient Necropolis of the city was placed.

View from the Portico of the Temple of Edfou (Edfu), Upper Egypt

This view... looking across the peristyle court of the Temple... is one of striking magnificence;... The cloistered corridor, covered with painted hieroglyphics, offered its shelter from an Egyptian sun to the priests and those permitted to enter the sacred precincts. The vast faces of the towers are covered with gigantic figures... and represent the offerings made by the Pharaohs to the gods. The holes which admitted light through the walls of these towers, served also to attach the staffs of the standards, from which in days of ceremony, the flags waved over 'the groups in procession. In the foreground... how enormous are these capitals! and yet how beautiful their structure!... The enormous stones, which rest upon and stretch from column to column, are among the wonders of Egyptian structure.

Façade of the Pronaos of the Temple of Edfou (Edfu)

...Around this cloister the priests ambulated, sheltered from the burning sun of Egypt, and where now a poor weaver is seen at work, shadowed by the screen which had sheltered the Pharaohs from the same sun – unchanged in its thousands of courses since the erection of the Temple; and unchanged in its effects and influences from a period long antecedent to the existence of any temple, any people, any social state in the land of Egypt. There are no ruins so complete in the valley of the Nile as those of Edfou, none by which the decorative taste of its architects can be so justly appreciated. Karnak is more severe than Dendera, more florid than Edfou – less severe than the former, this is more beautiful and pure than the latter. Not one of the temples of Egypt made a stronger impression for its beauty and picturesqueness upon our artist than that of Edfou.

Ruins of the Temple of Kom − Ombo, Upper Egypt

Of the Great Temple, much is concealed by vast sand drifts from the deserts; but enormous masses of its ruins rise above the arid and herbless surface which surrounds them, giving to the scene a character of dreary desolation in keeping with the decay of this once magnificent structure. The vast size of the stones of this Temple has struck every traveller;... as these masses lie about in utter confusion, they suggest the queries, by what power were they transported hither − erected − and have been displaced?... Every exposed spot on column or cornice is covered with hieroglyphics, and the Temple once bore on its surface the records of its own history.

Island of Philae, looking down the Nile

This beautiful Island, and the objects which enrich it, seen from any point of view, furnish a subject to the artist;... Beauty is its characteristic; for however much the ancient structures of Egypt may, by their vastness and extent, and the magnitude of their composing parts, cause us to reflect upon the powers employed to construct and arrange them, and thus impress us deeply with emotions of the sublime – in beauty, Philae, with its temples, has no rival on its sacred river.

In this view the masses of granite are seen which are covered with sculptured inscriptions, the beautiful hypaethral Temple, the obelisk... part of the cloistered court, ..., towering over all, the great propylon. ...the usual harbour where the boats of travellers are secured, ... granitic rocks and ruined temples, ...and the refreshing verdure of the palms and sycamores, contrasted with the arid and burning sands, ...give an air of enchantment to this spot, selected for the eternal repose of Osiris, ...who sleeps in Philae.

Asouan (Aswan) and the Island of Elephantine

Asouan was the ancient Syene;... There are few ruins of the ancient city remaining, and nothing of the Pharaonic or Ptolemaic periods... The most interesting objects in the neighbourhood of Asouan are the syenite and granite quarries, which supplied the vast demand of Egypt, in ancient times, for obelisks, columns and other massive requisites for their temples.

Elephantine, or, as it was sometimes called the Island of Flowers, lies on the Nile... not far from the Cataracts, which form the limit to Egypt on the borders of Nubia... The island... was covered by many magnificent structures... of these little now remains and the sand is fast covering the southern end of the island... Elephantine was a garrison position on the frontier of Egypt... It is now inhabited by Nubians.

Grand Portico of the Temple of Philae, Nubia

"Many parts of this building, particularly the portico, though not possessing the chaste and simple style of the Pharaonic monuments are remarkable for lightness and elegance;" ...In its use here exquisite taste has been displayed in design and arrangement... and so perfect is the colouring that remains to us... that we are aided to imagine what the effect must have been in the structure of Thebes... Under the cove of the cornice, and immediately over the grand entrance, is the winged sphere, the attribute of Athor... The rest of the ceiling is spangled with gold stars upon a blue ground: and the effect, together with the elaborate carving of the walls and columns, is very magnificent.

General View of Kalábshee, formerly Talmis, Nubia

This point of view admirably represents the striking situation of one of the largest of the Temples of Nubia. Its noble elevation above the river, the two magnificent terraces and steps by which the entrance is approached, the grand range of mountains by which the scene is backed, the rich groves of palms and accacias in front, and even the mud houses of the population here, add to the striking grandeur of the Temple and the picturesque character of the whole scene.

The Temples of Aboo-Simbel (Abu-Simbel), from the Nile

The smallest of these Temples, and the nearest to the Nile, was dedicated to Isis, and is excavated about ninety feet into the rock. It was, during many ages the only one known there; for the accumulations of sand had so concealed the Great Temple of Osiris that it remained undiscovered till 1813... "There is no road to this Temple, which stands just over the river, and is entirely cut out of the rocky side of the mountain; it is in complete preservation. In front of the entrance are six colossal figures, that measure from the ground to the knee six feet and a half." ..."southward... four immense colossal statues, cut out of the rock, at a distance of about two hundred yards from the Temple... are now almost entirely buried beneath the sands." — "on the wall of the rock, in the centre of the four statues, is a figure of the hawk-headed Osiris surmounted by a globe; beneath which, ...could the sand be cleared away, a vast Temple would be discovered."

(Belzoni removed enough of the sand to effect an entrance, and disclosed one of the most perfect and extraordinary works of the ancient Egyptians.)

Interior of the Great Temple of Aboo-Simbel (Abu Simbel), Nubia

"On descending into the splendid hall, ...a double row is seen of colossal figures, representing Remeses the Great, attached to square pillars, which appear to support the roof; the placid expression of these statues is still finer than that of the colossi without. There are four on each side, their arms crossed on their breasts, and bearing in their hands the crook and the scourge − emblems of government or power; those on one side wear the high conical cap, and on the other what is called the corn-measure.